# eat smart

# Fruit

**Vic Parker**

## Ask an adult for help

Always ask an adult to help you make the recipes and get all the ingredients and equipment ready. Remember to wash your hands before you start.

Quarto is the authority on a wide range of topics.

Quarto educates, entertains and enriches the lives of our readers—enthusiasts and lovers of hands-on living.

www.quartoknows.com

First published in hardback in the UK in 2017 by
QED Publishing
Part of The Quarto Group
The Old Brewery, 6 Blundell Street,
London, N7 9BH

A catalogue record for this book is available from the British Library.

ISBN 978 1 78493 720 1

Printed and bound in China

**Publisher:** Maxime Boucknooghe
**Editorial Director:** Victoria Garrard
**Art Director:** Miranda Snow
**Design and Editorial:** Starry Dog Books Ltd
**Consultant:** Charlotte Stirling-Reed BSc (hons), MSc, RNutr (Public Health)

**Picture credits**
(t=top, b=bottom, l=left, r=right, c=centre, fc=front cover)

**Alamy** 5tr Blickwinkel, 12cl Stuart Forster, 14cl Per Karlsson – BKWine.com

**Corbis** 14bl Jack K Clark

**Photolibrary** 9br Foodpix, 12bl Douglas Peebles, 13cr Raymond Forbes, 21tl A.J.J. Estudi

**Rex Features** 13tl Sipa Press

**Shutterstock** fc Eric Gevaert, fc Olga Danylenko, fc AlenKadr, fc Evgeny Karandaev, 4tl Valentyn Volkov, 4tr Andrjuss, 4bl Zloneg, 4bc Eric Gevaert, 4br Andrjuss, 5tl Samo Trebizan, 5b Ricardo Manuel Silva de Sousa, 5br (tree) Vondelmol, 6bc sta, 6–7 Martine Oger, 7tl Pgallery, 7tr Anna Kucherova, 7c Whaldener Endo, 7bl Elena Schweitzer, 7br Andrjuss, 8tl Khomulo Anna, 8tr grintan, 8cl Antonio Munoz Palomares, 8bl Branislav Senic, 8br Junial Enterprises, 9cl guy42, 11tl (strawberries)?, 11tr (orange) Valentyn Volkov, 11cl Maks Narodenko, 11cr (kiwi) Tihis, 11bl (apple) Bliznetsov, 11bl (banana) Yasonya, 11bc Victor Burnside, 11bc (plums) Yasonya, 11bc (strawberries)?, 12tr Yasonya, 12cr Alex Kuzovlev, 13b Christopher Elwell, 14tr Andrjuss, 14cr Riekephotos, 15tl Carolina K Smith, 15cl Morgan Lane Photography, 15cr Ultimathule, 15bl Lepas, 15bc Konstantynov, 15br Andrjuss, 19bl Stephen Aaron Rees, 19br (strawberries)?, 20tr Zloneg, 20cl Paul Prescott, 20br Christopher Elwell, 21tc (beefsteak) Oliver Hoffmann, 21tr Yellowj, 21cl Guy Erwood, 21br eAlisa.

**Public domain**
9tr&cr

## Words in **bold** are explained in the glossary on page 22.

# Contents

# Fruit

Some plants produce fruit, which contain the seeds of the plant. Fruits are often delicious to eat.

Grapes

Oranges

There are many different varieties of fruit, such as oranges, grapes, bananas, strawberries and tomatoes.

Bananas

Tomatoes

Strawberries

# Grow a blueberry plant

You will need:

- Young blueberry plant
- 30- or 40-cm-wide plant pot
- Ericaceous, or acidic, compost and fertilizer
- Watering can

1. Ask an adult if you can buy a young blueberry plant from a garden centre.

2. Put some ericaceous **compost** into the bottom of a 30- or 40-cm-wide plant pot. Carefully re-pot your plant into the bigger pot. Fill the gaps around the plant with more compost.

3. Water your plant well with rainwater. Keep the soil damp by watering it often.

4. In the spring, ask an adult to help you feed your plant with **fertilizer**. In the summer, pick and eat your own blueberries!

Some fruits, such as blackcurrants, grow on bushes. Other fruits, such as pomegranates and apples, grow on trees.

A pomegranate fruit has hundreds of seeds inside.

5

# Fruits around the world

## Different types of fruit are grown around the world.

Fruit need the right conditions in order to grow. Lots of fruits need warm sunshine to ripen them.

North America

Tomatoes grow well in warm climates. A lot of tomatoes are grown in the United States of America and Mexico.

South America

Guavas grow well in hot places that get lots of rain, such as Central America and northern South America.

Grapes and oranges grow well in southern Europe, where summers are warm and dry.

Plum trees can survive very cold winters. Lots of plums are grown in Russia and China.

Farmers have grown lychees in China since ancient times.

Europe

Asia

Bananas grow in hot, wet climates. India grows more bananas than any other country.

Africa

Oceania

Dates grow well in hot, dry places. Most of the world's dates are grown in north Africa and southwest Asia.

# Fruit in meals

Many fruits taste good hot or cold. You can also eat them frozen, dried or tinned.

It's healthy to drink one small glass of unsweetened fruit juice mixed with water a day.

At breakfast, we can add fresh berries to yoghurt or eat dried fruits, such as raisins, in muesli.

For lunch, we might eat a cheese and tomato sandwich.

After lunch, we could have a fruit salad.

## Ingredients:

- 255 g mango chunks cut from 2 to 3 ripe mangoes
- 285 g Greek yoghurt

Makes: 4 to 6 servings

# Make a mango sorbet

**1** Ask an adult to peel two or three ripe mangoes and cut the fruit from the stones. Put the fruit into a blender and blend until it forms a thick paste.

**2** Pour the mango paste into a bowl and stir in the yoghurt.

**3** Pour the mixture into a shallow tray and freeze it for two hours, then blend it again. Refreeze the mixture until it is firm. Serve and enjoy!

Some fruits, such as oranges, need peeling before you eat them. Other fruits, such as plums and apples, have tasty skin. Always wash fruits that don't need peeling.

Fruit can be made into jams, smoothies and puddings.

9

# Fruits for a healthy body

Fresh fruit contains **fibre**, minerals and vitamins, which keep us healthy.

Most fruits contain soluble fibre, which helps to keep our **digestive system** healthy.

Oranges contain Vitamin C, which helps our bodies to **absorb** iron from food. It also helps our bodies to heal.

Some fruits, such as bananas, contain potassium. This mineral helps to keep our **blood pressure** healthy.

Strawberries

Red fruits, such as strawberries, contain antioxidants. These help to protect the cells in our bodies.

Oranges

The vitamin C in oranges helps to keep our skin healthy.

Blueberries

The antioxidants in blueberries may help to keep our brains, eyes and heart healthy.

Kiwis

## Food fact

To stay healthy, we should eat at least five portions of different fruits and vegetables a day.

As well as being high in fibre and vitamins, kiwis also contain copper. This mineral helps our bones to grow when we are young.

# Growing bananas

Bananas

Banana plants need a warm, wet climate and lots of space to grow.

**1** A banana plant is grown from a shoot or sucker that has been cut from the base of a bigger banana plant.

After two months, a large bud grows from the leaves. This bud opens into groups of small flowers. **2**

**3** It takes four months for the flowers to turn into bananas. The bananas grow in groups, or hands, of 10 to 20 fruit.

After nine months, when the bananas are still green, the farmers cut them from the plants. **4**

The bananas are washed, boxed and kept cold so they don't ripen too soon. Then they are taken to shops to be sold. In the shops, the heat makes them ripen and turn yellow. **5**

## Ingredients:
- 1 scoop of plain frozen yoghurt
- 1 banana
- 50 g fruit, such as strawberries

Makes: 1 serving

## Make a banana split

**1** Put a scoop of plain frozen yoghurt into a bowl.

**2** Cut the banana down the middle and place the two long pieces on either side of the frozen yoghurt.

**3** Sprinkle with strawberries and serve.

13

# Growing grapes

Grapes

Grapes grow on plants called vines. The land where they are grown is a **vineyard**.

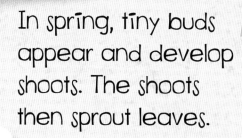

**1** New plants are grown from **cuttings** taken from the branches of older plants. The vines are planted in rows.

In spring, tiny buds appear and develop shoots. The shoots then sprout leaves.

**2**

**3** About two months after the buds appear, small groups of flowers grow on the shoots. The flowers turn into grapes.

14

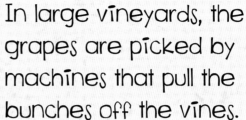

**4** In large vineyards, the grapes are picked by machines that pull the bunches off the vines.

In autumn, the leaves turn red and golden, and fall off. The bare branches are pruned, or cut back, in winter.

**5**

**6** Grapes are sold in fresh bunches or are dried to make raisins and currants. They are also made into grape juice and wine.

Raisins          Currants

### Food fact
Grapes first appear on a vine when the plant is three years old. The vine can go on producing grapes for 50 or even 100 years.

# Make fruity flapjacks

## Ingredients:

- 100 g butter, plus a little extra for greasing
- 3 tbsp golden syrup
- 100 g honey
- 200 g oats
- 75 g dried fruits such as raisins or apricots or a mixture of both

Makes: 12 to 15 portions

Use dried fruits to make these delicious, chewy flapjacks.

**1** Ask an adult to set the oven to 180°C/350°F/Gas 4. Grease a baking tray with butter. Then line it with some baking paper.

**2** Ask an adult to melt the butter, golden syrup and honey in a saucepan. Stir in the oats until they are evenly coated.

16

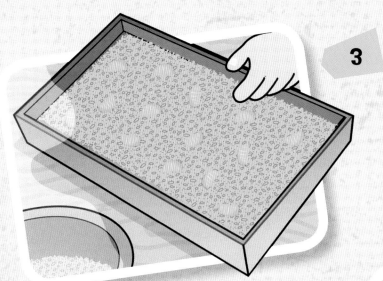

3. Tip half of the mixture into the tray. Press it into the corners. Sprinkle on the dried fruits, then spread the remaining mixture on top.

Ask an adult to put the tray into the oven. Bake for 15 to 20 minutes until the mixture is lightly browned.

4.

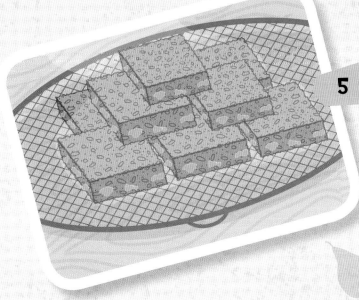

5. Ask an adult to cut the flapjack into portions in the tray while it is still hot, and to put the pieces on a wire rack to cool. Serve your delicious, fruity treats.

# Grow some strawberries

## Strawberries are easy to grow and everyone loves them!

**You will need:**

- Some pieces of broken crockery
- A strawberry pot
- Compost
- A strawberry plant for each hole in the strawberry pot
- A watering can

In spring, put some broken crockery into an empty strawberry pot. This will help water to drain from the soil. Fill the pot with compost up to the first holes.

**1**

**2**

Place your strawberry plants on the compost, with the leaves sticking out of each hole. Fill the pot with compost up to the next set of holes.

18

**3**
Continue planting until the pot is full. Place the pot in a sunny spot and water the plants regularly.

**4**

After about two months, small, white flowers will appear. Then strawberries will start to grow. They start off green, but then turn red and are ready to pick.

### Food fact
Strawberries are the only fruit with seeds on the outside.

# Growing tomatoes

Tomato plants need lots of sun to ripen their juicy red fruits.

Tomatoes

**1** In cool places, farmers sow tomato seeds in pots inside warm **polytunnels**. In warmer places, the seeds can be planted outdoors.

The seedlings need plenty of water to grow. Some farmers feed their young plants with fertilizer to help them grow big and strong.

**2**

Beefsteak tomato

Vine tomatoes

Plum tomato

Cherry tomatoes

## Food fact

Beefsteak, plum, cherry and vine tomatoes all taste quite different. Try them and see!

**3** As the plants get taller, the farmer ties them to canes to keep them upright. The plants produce yellow flowers, followed by little green tomatoes.

Tomatoes are usually picked when they are still green and unripe. This is so they stay fresh while they are taken to shops and factories, where they ripen.

**4**

# Glossary

## Absorb
To take something in.

## Blood pressure
A measure of how easily blood is flowing through our bodies.

## Compost
Rotting plant material that is full of goodness. It is added to soil to improve its quality.

## Cuttings
Pieces that have been cut from a plant's stem and put into the soil or water so they grow into new plants.

## Digestive system
All the parts of our body that are involved in breaking down and using food, and getting rid of waste products.

## Fertilizer
A substance that is spread onto the soil or mixed with water and given to plants to make them grow well.

## Fibre
Fibre is the part of plants that our bodies cannot digest. There are two types of fibre – insoluble and soluble. Both types are important for a healthy, balanced diet. Insoluble fibre makes it easier for our bodies to get rid of waste food. Soluble fibre helps to keep our digestive system healthy.

## Polytunnel
A curved metal frame covered in sheets of plastic to make a tunnel, a bit like a tent. Seeds or young plants are grown inside the tunnel to protect them from cold weather.

## Vineyard
A piece of land on which lots of grapevines are grown.

# Index

# Next Steps

❀ Show the children a variety of fruits. Talk about their size, shape, colour and texture.

❀ Find photographs of what different fruits look like when they are growing. Choose one to draw, and then label the different parts of the plant (roots, stem, leaves and fruit).

❀ Talk about how we eat fruits. Do we eat the skin? Should we eat the seeds? Show other forms that the fruit comes in, such as dried, tinned and frozen.

❀ Discuss why our bodies need fruit to stay healthy, and why it's best to eat different varieties. Explain that it is recommended we eat five portions of fruit and vegetables a day.

❀ Talk about which local fruits are ripe in different seasons.

❀ Ask the children to keep a fruit diary for a week to see how much fruit, and which types, they eat each day. Suggest ways they could include fruit in their breakfasts, snacks and puddings.

❀ Collect the packaging from various fruits bought in shops. On a map mark the countries where they came from. Talk about how far the fruits have travelled to reach the shops.

❀ Talk about why it is better to buy and eat fruit that has been grown locally. Suggest ways that it might help local people, and be better for the planet.

❀ Talk about how we might use different types of fruit in cooking. Make an international fruit cookbook with recipes and pictures from around the world.